Talking about time

How long does it take?

Jilly Attwood

Heinemann
LIBRARY

Little Nippers

www.heinemann.co.uk/library
Visit our website to find out more information about **Heinemann Library** books.

To order:
☎ Phone 44 (0) 1865 888066
🖹 Send a fax to 44 (0) 1865 314091
🖥 Visit the Heinemann Bookshop at www.heinemann.co.uk/library to browse our catalogue and order online.

First published in Great Britain by Heinemann Library, Halley Court, Jordan Hill, Oxford OX2 8EJ, part of Harcourt Education.
Heinemann is a registered trademark of Harcourt Education Ltd.

Editorial: Kathy Peltan and Kate Bellamy
Design: Jo Hinton-Malivoire and bigtop, Bicester, UK
Picture Research: Ruth Blair
Production: Séverine Ribierre

Originated by Dot Gradations Ltd
Printed and bound in China by South China Printing Company

ISBN 0 431 07939 0 (hardback)
09 08 07 06 05
10 9 8 7 6 5 4 3 2 1

ISBN 0 431 07944 7 (paperback)
09 08 07 06 05
10 9 8 7 6 5 4 3 2 1

British Library Cataloguing in Publication Data
Attwood, Jilly
529.7
Talking about time: How long does it take?
A full catalogue record for this book is available from the British Library.

Acknowledgements
The publishers would like to thank the following for permission to reproduce photographs: Alamy p. **18**; Corbis pp. **13**, **23b** (Lester Lefkowitz), **19** (Ariel Skelley), **7** (Larry Williams), **12**, **23a** (Jennie Woodcock/ Refections Photolibrary); Harcourt Education pp. **10-11**, **20**, **21** (Gareth Boden), **15** (Trevor Clifford), **8** (Chris Honeywell); Tudor Photography pp. **9**, **16**, **17**, **14**.

Cover photograph of children running , reproduced with permission of Corbis (Tom and Dee Ann McCarthy).

Our thanks to Annie Davy for her assistance in the preparation of this book.

Every effort has been made to contact copyright holders of any material reproduced in this book. Any omissions will be rectified in subsequent printings if notice is given to the publishers.

The paper used to print this book comes from sustainable resources.

Contents

Getting ready for school

Niran is zipping up his jacket.

Zip!

4

Next he buttons up his coat.
Which takes longer?

5

Going to school

David and his mum and sister are walking to school.

At the sand tray

George has a
big bucket.

Jenny has a
small bucket.

Which bucket will be
quickest to fill with sand?

George filled his bucket quickly.
But Jenny was quicker.

Playtime

Does it take longer to climb up or to slide down?

Wheeee!

Sports day

Who will win the race?

Which is fastest,
a running race or a sack race?

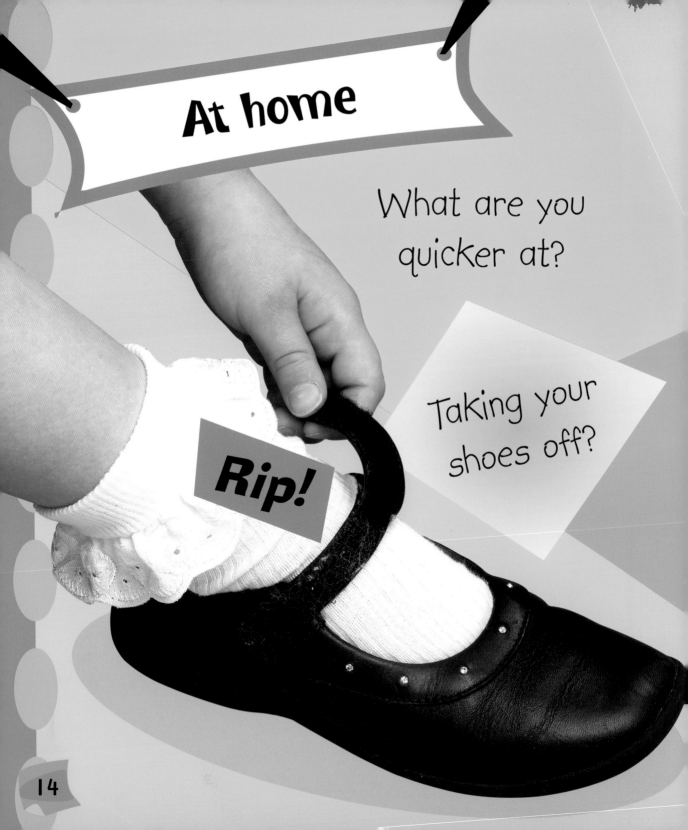

Or putting them on?

Baking

These children are helping to make bread. Have you made bread?

stir!

It takes longer to make bread
than to eat bread!

Doggy time

Peter is brushing his dog.

18

David is washing his dog.

Which takes the longest time?
Brushing or washing?

Bedtime

Sheryl is brushing her teeth and washing her face.

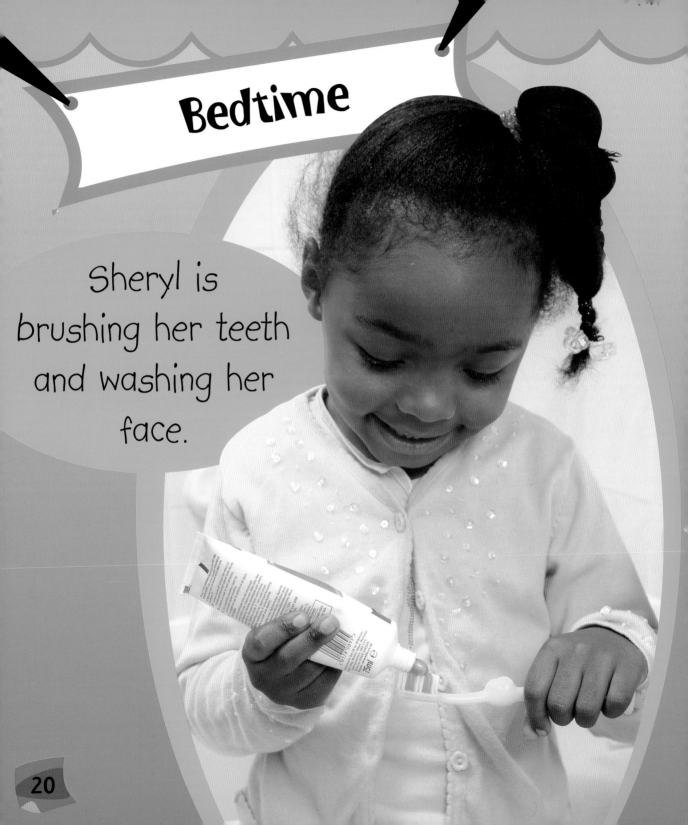

Which takes the longest time?
Brushing or washing?

How long does it take?

Which takes the longest?
Which takes the shortest?

OR

OR

OR

Index

Notes for adults

The *Talking about time* series introduces young children to the concept of time. By relating their own experiences to specific moments in time, the children can start to explore the pattern of regular events that occur in a day, week or year. The following Early Learning Goals are relevant to this series:

Knowledge and understanding of the world
Early learning goals for a sense of time
• find out about past and present events in their own lives, and in those of their families and other people they know
Early learning goals for exploration and investigation
• look closely at similarities, differences, patterns and change
Early learning goals for cultures and beliefs
• describe significant events for family or friends

Mathematical development
• use quantitative language in comparisons

This book explores the passing of time of activities familiar to children. For each set of activities it asks the reader to consider which of the two takes the longer or shorter time to do. The book provides an opportunity for children, in a classroom or home situation, to try out the activities for themselves to consolidate their understanding of concepts associated with time such as *longer/longest*, *quicker/quickest*, *fastest*, *shortest*.

Follow-up activities
• Use a stop-watch to measure how long it takes a child to do various linked activities, e.g. zipping up a jacket and buttoning up a jacket; climbing up a slide and sliding down it.
• Before filling up different-sized containers, such as buckets, with sand, ask your child to predict which ones will take the longest and shortest time to fill up and why.